RAF, DOMINION & ALLIED SQUADRONS AT WAR:
STUDY, HISTORY AND STATISTICS

COMPILED BY
PHIL H. LISTEMANN

Drawings by Claveworks Classics

PREFACE

The purpose of this study is to provide aviation historians and enthusiasts with a range of information relative to each of the Commonwealth squadrons that saw combat during World War II. Each record will comprise a short history, complete with illustrations and artwork, and accompanied by the following appendices:

Appendix I: Squadron Commanders and Flight Commanders
Appendix II: Major awards
Appendix III: Operational diary (number of sorties per month)
Appendix IV: Victory list
Appendix V: Aircraft losses on operations
Appendix VI: Aircraft losses in accidents
Appendix VII: Aircraft Serial numbers matching with individual letters (including mission totals for multi-engine aircraft)
Appendix VIII: Nominal roll (Captains only for bomber and seaplane units)
Appendix IX: Roll of Honour

Individual files will be constantly updated, when any fresh information comes to light. Additional information will be available for download, at no charge, on each squadron's site at:

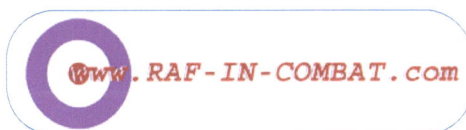

www.RAF-IN-COMBAT.com

GLOSSARY OF TERMS

RANKS

AC: Aircraftman
G/C: Group Captain
W/C: Wing Commander
S/L: Squadron Leader
F/L: Flight Lieutenant
F/O: Flying Officer
P/O: Pilot Officer
W/O: Warrant Officer
F/Sgt: Flight Sergeant
Sgt: Sergeant
Cpl: Corporal
LAC: Leading Aircraftman

OTHER

AAF: Auxiliary Air Force
CO: Commanding Officer
DFC: Distinguished Flying Cross

DFM: Distinguished Flying Medal
DSO: Distinguished Service Order
Eva.: Evaded
Inj.: Injured
ORB: Operational Record Book
OTU: Operational Training Unit
PAF: Polish Air Force
PoW: Prisoner of War
RAF: Royal Air Force
RAAF: Royal Australian Air Force
RCAF: Royal Canadian Air Force
RNZAF: Royal New Zealand Air Force
SAAF: South African Air Force
Sqn: Squadron
TOC: Taken on charge
†: Killed

No. 121 (Eagle) Squadron 1941-1942

ISBN: 978-2-918590-72-9

Contributors & Acknowledgments:
Paul Sortehaug.

Cover : Spitfire Mk.VB BM590 flying over the British countryside in summer 1942.

MAIN EQUIPMENT

HURRICANE I	**May.41 - Jul.41**
HURRICANE II	**Jul.41 - Nov.41**
SPITFIRE II	**Oct.41 - Nov.41**
SPITFIRE V	**Nov.41 - Sep.42**

SQUADRON CODE LETTERS:

AV

SQUADRON HISTORY

No.121 Squadron, the second of the three 'Eagle' squadrons to be manned by American volunteer pilots, was re-formed [1] at Kirton-in-Lindsey on **14 May 1941**. Working-up on Hurricane Is, it had re-equipped with Mk. IIBs before becoming operational at the end of July. The first sortie was flown by F/L Hugh Kennard on 2 August, an uneventful Scramble. Operational activity was relatively quiet over the following six months with the squadron being employed on just routine East Coast Convoy Patrols and a few Scrambles. During this period though the squadron was able to make its first claim, a probable Ju88 on 8 August, shared by Pilot Officer Selder Edner and Sergeant Jack Mooney; these pilots were destined to become the most successful members of the squadron during its short existence. The first claim was followed by another, ten days later, by the CO himself. Thereafter it was a wait of seven months before another score was made, by which time the squadron had branched out offensively, performing its first Rhubarb and Sweeps. During this time it was based at North Weald and was flying Spitfire Mk.Vs, having upgraded from ageing Spitfire Mk.IIs, with which it had been equipped for just a matter of weeks.

The real war began, for 121 Squadron, from December 1941 onwards, with operations increasing in intensity, the high-point coming early in 1942 with the operation against the German warships, *Scharnhorst*, *Gneisenau* and *Prinz Eugen*, as they made their dash through the Channel. With the increase in activity, so too did the squadron's tally, and among the pilots who distinguished themselves were Selder Edner, Jack Mooney, 'Barry' Mahon and Jim Daley. During the summer of 1942, the squadron was fully employed on Channel Sweeps and Bomber Escorts with an occasional Roadstead as well. Its last major assignment was supporting the Dieppe raid, during which it claimed two confirmed victories and a probable for the loss of four aircraft and three pilots, one of whom became a prisoner of war.

One month later, 27 September, F/L Jim Daley led a Shipping Recco, and upon landing at 17.40, signed off the last operation under RAF management. Two days later, on **29 September 1942**, the squadron was transferred to the U.S. Army Air Corps, as 335th FS of the 4th FG, at Debden. During its 16 month existence 121 Squadron had claimed 26 aircraft destroyed or probably destroyed in over 3,100 sorties. This was achieved for the loss of 21 aircraft on operations, with 11 pilots killed in action and three reported prisoners of war. An additional three pilots were lost in accidents. Of the three Eagle squadrons, it was the only one not to have an American appointee as CO while with the RAF.

[1] *No.121 Sqn was first formed in January 1918 and was disbanded in August the same year.*

SQUADRON BASES

Kirton-in-Lindsey	05.05.41 - 28.09.41	North Weald	16.12.41 - 03.01.42
Digby	28.09.41 - 03.10.41	Southend	03.01.42 - 23.09.42
Kirton-in-Lindsey	03.10.41 - 16.12.41	Debden	23.09.42 - 29.09.42

Recruting Pilots

Shoulder badge of American volunteers serving one of the Eagle Squadrons.

Shoulder badge of American volunteers for officers. The Eagle pilots were actually a tiny part of the Americans who served the RAF and RCAF during the war.

From the very beginning of the war in Europe Americans, at all levels, took an interest, realising that, sooner or later, they would be involved. Creating a fighter squadron comprising American volunteers quickly took root in certain minds, including Charles Sweeny's, an ex-serviceman of the French Foreign Legion during World War One. He was one who had been inspired by the exploits of the famous Lafayette squadron, manned by Americans, and the status it held, all of which had been portrayed by the media of that time.

He established a network, allowing interested Americans to cross the Atlantic, to support France, although French enthusiasm on this occasion was not so positive. Compounding Sweeny's problems was a Congress Neutrality Act, voted in 1935 and revised and reinforced many times thereafter, making the recruiting of American volunteers for fighting in Foreign countries very difficult indeed. The US authorities closely monitored activity of this nature and would not facilitate any enlistment. Volunteers, or for that matter anyone suspected as being one, would be detained at the Canadian border, this situation existing right up until the fall of France in June 1940. As a result volunteers arrived too late, and the French overwhelmed by their own situation had little to offer them. Consequently the vast majority disappeared amid the upheaval, either killed or made prisoners, while others returned to the USA by their own means. Only five of the original volunteers are known to have arrived in Great Britain.

Thereafter the situation changed and American authorities became more accommodating. At the same time the number of volunteers increased, since many were aware that the USA was readying to enter the war. The Knight Committee, from the name of its founder, was set up and this organisation would be responsible for the bulk of American recruitment, starting in the spring of 1940. In August 1941 this committee became the Canadian Aviation Bureau, before being disbanded late in 1942. Some 250 American pilots would serve with three American fighter units - the Eagle Squadrons - formed in the RAF between 1940 and 1942. These though were only a fraction of the hundreds, who passed through the committee, to enrol in the RAF or the RCAF, and fight under the RAF umbrella in Europe, the Middle East and the Far East. Their motives were varied, but the majority simply sought adventure. Their aspirations were to become pilots but they had been refused entry into their own country's air arms, on educational, competency or medical grounds. Both the RCAF and the RAF (Royal Air Force Volunteer Reserve - RAFVR) provided viable alternatives, and the prospect of flying a Spitfire, by then the best Allied fighter, only added to reinforce their desire to join up.

The American pilots, in particular those that served with the Eagle Squadrons, were to benefit from certain privileges. Most were not required to pledge allegiance to the King, upon their engagement, and thus were able to maintain their American citizenship. Additionally, it was understood that, those passed by the Knight Committee would be commissioned at the end of their training, as opposed to the majority of those who joined the RCAF, who graduated as Non-Commissioned Officers. This disparity was to create problems when the integration of these pilots into the Army Air Force took place.

Transfer to the AAF

The Transfer of personnel to the AAF, a natural outcome, was not so simple for numerous reasons. Firstly, the RAF had put a considerable investment into their training, and they were fully operational, and doing a fine job, when America entered the war in December 1941. The British simply were not in a hurry to disband the three American fighter squadrons. The pilots themselves had signed up with the RAFVR, that is, until the end of the war, and adding to English woes, they now faced war on a new front with Japan. Integration into the AAF meant that the pilots trained by the RAF would, sooner or later, come into contact with countrymen trained in American schools, and this would not be to everyone's satisfaction. At certain levels 'Eagle' flyers had been subjected to a British influence, not always well embraced by Americans.

Rank equivalence also posed problems. The AAF did not have anyone below the base rank of Second Lieutenant as a pilot. NCOs transferring from the RCAF would automatically have to become Second Lieutenants. The situation involving officers was relatively straight forward - they would acquire the comparative rank. There was also debate about how these transferees should be utilised. 8th Air Force officials of rank felt that it would be logical to divide these pilots amongst AAF units arriving in England, where their solid experience would be of some benefit.

Others were of the opinion that the three Eagle squadrons, having established a fine reputation and not wishing to separate, should be forged into a specific unit - the 4th Fighter Group. In effect this was what happened in September of 1942. However some pilots chose to remain in the RAF, out of loyalty and feeling the change would not be in their best interests.

As for the 4th FG it was to keep its unique identity for the early months of it's existence, but by the summer of 1943, due to losses and manpower turnover, it would become an American Fighter Group, falling in line with all the others.

For those who choose to integrate into the AAF, it was not immediately apparent whether they had made the correct choice or not. While they gained a pay increase and access to an array of typically American luxuries, they lost an element of prestige with the British population who held them in high regard - they were considered to be a cut above the average American.There was also the loss of spirit and friendship, very present within the British units, which became more obvious with the arrival of American pilots coming from the USA, replacing those who were lost or had left.

The pilots of the Eagle Squadrons were special, being volunteers in a British war that was not theirs and, for political reasons, they had been courted by and received a great deal of press. Once integration into the AAF had taken place, this became something of a burden. The AAF moved quickly to tone down their amount of press coverage so that they would become less conspicuous, for both morale and political reasons.

Shoulder badge of American volunteers serving the RCAF.

Variant of shoulder badge for American volunteers.

APPENDIX I
SQUADRON AND FLIGHT COMMANDERS

Rank and Name	SN	Origin	Dates
S/L Robin P.R. **POWELL**	RAF No.33278	RAF	14.05.41 - 17.01.42
S/L Hugh C. **KENNARD**	RAF No.40396	RAF	17.01.42 - 31.07.42
S/L William D. **WILLIAMS**	RAF No.78985	RAF	02.08.42 - 29.09.42
A FLIGHT			
F/L Hugh C. **KENNARD**	RAF No.40396	RAF	14.05.41 - 17.01.42
F/L Vivian E. **WATKINS**	RAF No.64868	(US)/RAF	17.01.42 - 09.03.42
F/L Thomas W. **ALLEN** *(†)*	CAN./J.15015	(US)/RCAF	09.03.42 - 31.05.42
F/L John G. **DUFOUR**	RAF No.89765	(US)/RAF	09.06.42 - 28.06.42
F/L Selden R. **EDNER**	RAF No.64860	(US)/RAF	28.06.42 - 29.09.42
B FLIGHT			
F/L Royce C. **WILKINSON**	RAF No.44125	RAF	16.05.41 - 09.03.42
F/L Clarence L. **MARTIN**	RAF No.65975	(US)/RAF	09.03.42 - 19.05.42
F/L John J. **MOONEY** *(†)*	CAN./J.15024	(US)/RCAF	19.05.42 - 16.06.42
F/L William J. **DALEY**	RAF No.101457	(US)/RAF	20.06.42 - 29.09.42

APPENDIX II
MAJOR AWARDS

DSO: -

DFC: 4

William James **DALEY** (No.101457 - RAF), *USA*
Selden Raymond **EDNER** (No.64860 - RAF), *USA*
Hugh Charles **KENNARD** (No.40396 - RAF)
Jackson Barrett **MAHON** (No.108640 - RAF), *USA*

DFM: -

APPENDIX III
OPERATIONAL DIARY - NUMBER OF SORTIES PER MONTH

Date	Month	Total	Date	Month	Total
Aug-41	172	172			
Sep.41	84	256	Jun.42	330	2,113
Oct.41	69	325	Jul.42	548	2,661
Nov.41	96	421	Aug.42	302	2,963
Dec.41	65	486	Sep.42	168	3,131
Jan.42	135	621			
Feb.42	155	776	**Grand Total**	**3,131**	**3,131**
Mar.42	199	975			
Avr.42	426	1,401		Extracted from AIR27/914	
May.42	382	1,783			

APPENDIX IV
VICTORY LIST - CONFIRMED (C) AND PROBABLE (P) CLAIMS

Date	Pilot	SN	Origin	Type	Serial	Code	Nb	Cat.

HURRICANE II

Date	Pilot	SN	Origin	Type	Serial	Code	Nb	Cat.
08.08.41	P/O Selden R. **EDNER**	RAF No.64860	(US)/RAF	Ju88	**Z3427**	AV-R	0.5	P
	Sgt John J. **MOONEY**	CAN./R.56127	(US)/RCAF		**Z5058**	AV-E	0.5	P
18.08.41	S/L Robin P.R. **POWELL**	RAF No.33278	RAF	Bf109	**Z3493**		1.0	P

SPITFIRE V

Date	Pilot	SN	Origin	Type	Serial	Code	Nb	Cat.
23.03.42	P/O John J. **MOONEY**	CAN./J.15024	(US)/RCAF	Fw190	**AA904**	AV-W	1.0	C
24.03.42	P/O Reade F. **TILLEY**	CAN./J.15011	(US)/RCAF	Fw190	**AD463**		1.0	P
12.04.42	P/O LeRoy A. **SKINNER**	RAF No.101460	(US)/RAF	Fw190	**AD501**		1.0	C
	F/L Thomas W. **ALLEN**	CAN./J.15015	(US)/RCAF	Fw190	**BL986**		1.0	P
15.04.42	P/O LeRoy A. **SKINNER**	RAF No.101460	(US)/RAF	Fw190	**W3804**		1.0	C
	F/O Selden R. **EDNER**	RAF No.64860	(US)/RAF	Fw190	**AA903**	AV-N	1.0	C
27.04.42	P/O William J. **DALEY**	RAF No.101457	(US)/RAF	Ju52*	**P8794**	AV-Q	0.5	C
	P/O LeRoy A. **SKINNER**	RAF No.101460	(US)/RAF		**W3804**		0.5	C
17.05.42	P/O William J. **DALEY**	RAF No.101457	(US)/RAF	Fw190	**R6890**		1.0	C
	F/O Selden R. **EDNER**	RAF No.64860	(US)/RAF	Fw190	**AA903**	AV-N	1.0	C
27.05.42	P/O William J. **DALEY**	RAF No.101457	(US)/RAF	Bf109	**BL986**		1.0	C
08.06.42	F/L John J. **MOONEY**	CAN./J.15024	(US)/RCAF	Fw190	**AD423**		2.0	C
	P/O Jackson B. **MAHON**	RAF No.108640	(US)/RAF	Fw190	**?**		2.0	C
31.07.42	Sgt William P. **KELLY**	CAN./R.89902	(US)/RCAF	Bf109	**BM581**	AV-P	1.0	C
	P/O Frank R. **BOYLES**	RAF No.111571	(US)/RAF	Bf109	**AA841**		1.0	C
	F/L Selden R. **EDNER**	RAF No.64860	(US)/RAF	Fw190	**EN918**	AV-X	2.0	C
	P/O Jackson B. **MAHON**	RAF No.108640	(US)/RAF	Fw190	**BM405**	AV-J	2.0	C
	S/L Hugh C. **KENNARD**	RAF No.40396	RAF	Bf109	**BL234**		1.0	C
19.08.42	Sgt Leon McF. **BLANDING**	CAN./R.79288	(US)/RCAF	Fw190	**EN822**		1.0	P
	F/L Selden R. **EDNER**	RAF No.64860	(US)/RAF	Fw190	**EN918**	AV-X	1.0	C
	P/O Gilbert O. **HALSEY**	RAF No.112619	(US)/RAF	Fw190	**BM590**	AV-R	1.0	P

Actually a Junkers W34 but credited as a Ju52

Total: 26.0
Aircraft damaged: 16.0

APPENDIX V
AIRCRAFT LOST ON OPERATIONS

Date	Pilot	S/N	Origin	Serial	Code	Mark	Fate

HURRICANE

Date	Pilot	S/N	Origin	Serial	Code	Mark	Fate
02.10.41	F/Sgt Reade F. **TILLEY**	CAN./R.64276	(US)/RCAF	**Z5058**	AV-E	IIB	-

Took off at 17.30 for a dusk patrol. Engine failure in flight and baled out near Burton-on-Trent, Staffs. American from Florida and one of the original pilots, he later volunteered to serve overseas in Malta with Nos.601 & 126 Sqns and claimed 7 confirmed victories. He transferred to USAAF in October 1942. DFC [No.126 Sqn].

Note on the aircraft: TOC No.51 MU 02.07.41, issued to No.121 Sqn 19.07.41.

Spitfire

07.12.41 P/O Richard F. **Patterson** Can./J.2928 (us)/RCAF **W3711** AV-H VB †
Took off at 11.25 with P/O Vivan Watkins for a RHUBARB sortie near Blankenberge (Belgium). American from Virginia, he had arrived at the squadron in June.

Note on the aircraft: TOC No.9 MU 18.08.41, issued to No.121 Sqn 07.11.41. Previously served with No.603 Sqn.

12.12.41 P/O Kenneth LeR. **Holder** RAF No.118173 (us)/RAF **AA871** AV-D VB †
Took off with at 16.05 with 3 others for a convoy patrol and disappeared over the Channel, cause unknown. American from California, he had joined the squadron in September.

Note on the aircraft: TOC No.9 MU 25.10.41, presentation aircraft 'ROYAL TUNBRIDGE WELLS', issued to No.121 Sqn 05.11.41.

08.03.42 P/O William L.C. **Jones** Can./J.15052 (us)/RCAF **AB206** AV-S VB **PoW**
Took off at 15.00 with 11 others for a sweep over France, F/L Wilkinson leading. Heavy flak experienced and was shot down while between Cassel and Poperinge. Last seen under control with gycol pouring out. Later reported PoW at Stalag Luft III. American from Maryland he had served with the squadron since July 1941.

Note on the aircraft: TOC No.8 MU 02.01.42, presentation aircraft 'BIHAR VI', issued to No.121 Sqn 08.01.42.

09.03.42 P/O Roy W. **Evans** RAF No.108632 (us)/RAF **BL465** VB **Inj.**
Took off at 14.00 for a convoy patrol off Martlesham Heath with 7 others. On landing back, the pilot overshot the aerodrome, and the plane stalled and crashed. He sustained a fractured arm and broken jaw, rejoining the squadron in mid-june. American from Missouri, he transferred to USAAF in September 1942. Completed his tour with 4th FG, and was on a second with 359th FG when shot down on 14.02.45 in P-51D-15-NA 44-14894 and made PoW. Received credit for five victories.

Note on the aircraft: TOC No.12 MU 01.12.41, issued to No.121 Sqn 13.12.41 then to No.403 (RCAF) Sqn 31.12.41 before returning to No.121 Sqn 22.02.42.

24.03.42 P/O LeRoy A. **Skinner** RAF No.101460 (us)/RAF **BL963** VB -
Nine aircraft took off at 14.30 with the North Weald Wing (403 RCAF and 222 Sqns) to escort 8 Bostons to their target. The Squadron was flying at 15-16,000 feet when enemy aircraft showed up, On the way home, P/O Skinner made a crash landing at Deal owing to lack of petrol, escaping injuries. Became a PoW the following month with the squadron.

Note on the aircraft: TOC No.5 MU 17.02.42, issued to No.121 Sqn 13.03.42.

12.04.42 P/O Selden R. **Edner** RAF No.64860 (us)/RAF **BL447** VB -
Took off at 12.35 with 3 others for a sweep with the North Weald, Deben and Hornchurch Wings, S/L Kennard leading the 121 Sqn formation. Encountered FW190s and was damaged in ensuing combat. Aircraft was not repaired. American from Minnesota, who had been with the squadron since June 1941. Eventually transferred to USAAF in September 1942 continuing to fly with the 4th FG until shot down and made PoW on 08.03.44 while flying P-51B-5-NA 43-6462. After the war he remained in the Air Force and was kidnapped and excecuted during the Greek Civil War on 22 January 1949 while serving as a member of the US Military Assistance and Advisory Group (MAAG).

Note on the aircraft: TOC No.8 MU 26.02.42, issued to No.121 Sqn 14.03.42.

17.04.42 F/Sgt Frederick C. **Austin** Can./R.58580 (us)/RCAF **AD498** AV-C VB †
Took off 15.10 with 5 others for a sweep, the CO leading. Over the French coast near Boulogne, the formation was intercepted by FW190s, and he failed to return. American from California, he had arrived at the squadron the previous month, having served earlier with No.133 (Eagle) Sqn between December 1941 and March 1942.

Note on the aircraft: Presentation aircraft SOUTH WEST LANSASHIRE TOC No.24 MU 23.10.41, issued to No.121 Sqn 30.11.41.

25.04.42   P/O Bruce C. **Downs**   RAF No.108631   (US)/RAF   **AB793**   VB   -

Took off at 09.40 escorting six Bostons to Dunkirk with 11 others, CO leading. Formation intercepted enemy aircraft attacking the Bostons and in the ensuing melée pilot was shot down and was forced to bale out. Brought back to the squadron by P/O Stepp in a Magister. One month later he volunteered for overseas duty and served with No.126 Sqn in Malta and subsequently transferred to USAAF in September 1942.

Note on the aircraft: TOC No.45 MU date not recorded, issued to No.121 Sqn 21.04.42, from No.111 Sqn.

28.04.42   P/O Carl G. **Bodding**   RAF No.108628   (US)/RAF   **AD289**   AV-J   VB   †

Took off at 09.40 escorting six Bostons to Dunkirk with 11 others, CO leading. Formation intercepted enemy aircraft attacking the Bostons and in the ensuing melée pilot was shot down in flames and was forced to bale out a mile or two inland of Dunkirk. American from Kansas, he had joined the squadron the previous month, having been posted from No.133 (Eagle) Sqn with which he served between January and March 1942.

Note on the aircraft: TOC No.33 MU 21.09.41, issued to No.121 Sqn 15.11.41.

                P/O LeRoy A. **Skinner**   RAF No.101460   (US)/RAF   **W3804**   VB   **PoW**

As above. American from Missouri, who had served with the squadron since September 1941. Later reported as a PoW in Stalag Luft III.

Note on the aircraft: TOC No.39 MU 29.08.41, issued to No.121 Sqn 26.03.42, previoulsly with Nos.611 & 154 Sqns.

04.05.42   P/O Ralph W. **Freiberg**   RAF No.110340   (US)/RAF   **P8794**   AV-Q   VB   †

Took off for an escort of 6 Bostons to Le Havre (France) 09.50 with 11 others, the CO leading. Encountered enemy aircraft over target and pilot reported missing. His leader, F/L 'Whitey' Martin, saw him diving from 15,000 feet towards the sea about 15 miles off Le Havre, the aircraft apparently under control. American pilot from Minessota who joined the squadron in March.

Note on the aircraft: TOC No.39 MU 06.07.41, issued to No.121 Sqn 04.11.41. FH 144.7.

                P/O Robert V. **Brossmer**   RAF No.106352   (US)/RAF   **AD460**   AV-P   VB   †

As above. He was last seen by P/O John Mooney just after leaving the French coast. American from New York, who had been posted in March from No.133 Sqn, with whom he served between December 1941 and March 1942.

Note on the aircraft: TOC No.37 MU 17.10.41, issued to No.121 Sqn 04.11.41. FH 159.8.

31.05.42   F/L Thomas W. **Allen**   Can./J.15015   (US)/RCAF   **W3645**   VB   †

Took off from Martlesham at 15.15 for a Shipping Recco, CO leading. 4 miles north east of Walcherau, the CO saw 2 vessels of the minesweeper class and ordered the squadron to attack the foremost of the two. F/L Allen and his No.2 (Sgt Fred Vance) made two attacks on this ship. During the second attack F/L Allen's machine struck the water, and ricochet up to about 1,000 feet. He announced over the R/T that his aircraft was coming apart and that he proposed to ditch at 100 mph. He did so at a rather a steep glide and he was not seen to emerge from the Spitfire, which sank immediately. It is thought that he may have been hit in the engine during the second attack as P/O 'Barry' Mahon stated that he saw glycol streaming from Allen's aircraft. American pilot from South Carolina, who had served with the squadron since June 1941.

Note on the aircraft: TOC No.6 MU 01.08.41, presentation aircraft 'JOSEPH SMOUHA' renamed 'WAIKATO', issued to No.121 Sqn 30.04.42. previously with No.485 (NZ) Sqn.

16.06.42   F/L John J. **Mooney**   Can./J.15024   (US)/RCAF   **W3841**   VB   †

Took off at 12.20 for a RHUBARB sortie with F/O 'Sed' Edner. Travelling towards Ostend a freight train was observed. They attacked the train from astern, F/O Edner giving it a four-second burst. This resulted in it being brought to a standstill with the belief that the driver had been killed. Immediately after this attack F/L Mooney disappeared, so Edner called him on his R/T, but it had gone u/s. He then circled the train twice to see if there was any sign of F/L Mooney, but it was in vain. American pilot from New York he was posted to the squadron in June 1941 after a brief stay at No.71 Sqn.

Note on the aircraft: TOC No.45 MU 07.09.41, issued to No.121 Sqn 29.05.42, having flown with 501 & 72 sqns.

31.07.42   S/L Hugh C. **Kennard**   RAF No.40396   RAF   **BL234**   VB   **Inj.**

Took off at 14.15 for sweep over Abbeville with 11 others; E/A were sighted and attacked by the squadron. In the ensuing combat, S/L Kennard was injured in the knee, hand and buttocks and the aircraft seriously damaged. He was able to crash-land

at Lympne and was taken to Maidstone Hospital. S/L Kennard was a pre-war RAF officer and was serving with No.66 Sqn at the outbreak of war, then with No.610 Sqn before rejoining No.66 Sqn again in March 1940. He was then ordered to No.306 (Polish) Sqn as a Flight Commander, at the end of August 1940, before being posted to No.121 Sqn, in May 1941. When he was injured, his tally was four confirmed victories, three being shared, and he received the DFC whilst serving the squadron. After his injuries, he was given various non-flying postings until May 1945 when he took command of No.74 Sqn in Germany. He retired in December1957.
Note on the aircraft: TOC No.12 MU 28.11.41, issued to No.121 Sqn 31.12.41.

| | P/O Norman D. **YOUNG** | RAF No.116163 | (US)/RAF | **AA732** | | VB | † |

As above and reported missing from this operation. No details available. American pilot from Oregon, who had joined the unit just two weeks previously.
Note on the aircraft: TOC No.8 MU 12.09.41, issued to No.121 Sqn 01.06.42. Also with 485 (NZ), 609.

| **19.08.42** | P/O James LaR. **TAYLOR** | RAF No.110338 | (US)/RAF | **AD569** | | VB | † |

Took off at 08.40 to cover the Dieppe raid with ten others, F/L 'Sed' Edner leading. Missing after air combat with fighters, one of which he is believed to have collided with, over the target. American pilot from Indiana, who had served in the squadron since March.
Note on the aircraft: TOC No.9 MU 09.12.41, issued to No.121 Sqn 05.08.42. Also served with Nos.74, 133 (Eagle) and 401 (RCAF) Sqns.

| | P/O Jackson B. **MAHON** | RAF No.108640 | (US)/RAF | **BM405** | AV-J | VB | **PoW** |

As above. While patrolling at 5,000 feet encountered FW190s and was shot down. American pilot from California, who had arrived at the squadron during December 1941. Reported PoW at Stalag Luft III. Just before to be shot down he had claimed his fifth victory which could not be confirmed.
Note on the aircraft: TOC No.338 MU 03.04.42, issued to No.121 Sqn 17.06.42.

| | P/O Gene B. **FETROW** | RAF No.113977 | (US)/RAF | **BM401** | | VB | - |

As above. Severely damaged in air combat. Pilot was able to bring back his aircraft, which was on fire, to the British Isles, where he baled out. American pilot from California, who had been in the sqn since February 1942.
Note on the aircraft: TOC No.8 MU 24.04.42, issued to No.121 Sqn 05.05.42.

| | P/O Julian M. **OSBORNE** | RAF No.112312 | (US)/RAF | **P8589** | | VB | - |

Took off at 16.15 for a sweep to Dieppe, the third of the day, with the CO, William Williams, leading. While patrolling at 4,000 feet E/A came in from the clouds and fired at the squadron hitting Osborne's aircraft; his engine was set on fire but was able to land back in UK. American pilot from Virginia, who had been with the squadron since May. He transferred to USAAF in September 1942.
Note on the aircraft: Built as M.IIB, TOC No.45 MU 08.06.41, presentation aircraft 'MAKASSAR' and served with Nos.65 & 616 before being converted to VB and issued to No.121 Sqn 05.06.42.

| **21.09.42** | P/O John T. **SLATER** | RAF No.116645 | (US)/RAF | **P8339** | AV-I | VB | † |

Took off at 14.55 for a shipping recce to Haastede with P/O William Kelly. Shot up one Flak ship, which was left burning, but was hit in glycol tank and seen to crash into the sea. American from New Jersey who had been in the squadron since June. As per 121 ORB as Slater is offically a USAAF loss as O-885133, having made his transfer on 16 September.
Note on the aircraft: Built as M.IIB, TOC No.45 MU 24.04.41, presentation aircraft 'MADURA' and served with No.145 Sqn before being converted to VB and issued to No.121 Sqn 15.03.42.

Total: 21

APPENDIX VI
AIRCRAFT LOST IN ACCIDENTS

HURRICANE

15.06.41   P/O Richard F. **PATTERSON**   CAN./J.2928   (US)/RCAF   **V7604**   I   -

Engine cut during a training flight and abandoned over Old Leake, 3.5 m NE of Boston, Lincs. Posted in just five days earlier. Subsequently killed with the squadron (see entry 07.12.41). American from Virginia.

Note on the aircraft: TOC No.15 MU 20.10.40. Issued No.121 Sqn 15.05.41. Served previously with 46 Sqn.

21.06.41   P/O Loran L. **LAUGHLIN**   RAF No.61925   (US)/RAF   **P3097**   I   †

Dived into ground 2 m NW of Scampton during a training flight, cause unknown. American fromTexas and a squadron founder member.

Note on the aircraft: TOC No.22 MU 15.06.40. Issued No.121 Sqn 15.05.41. Served previously with No.245 & 46 Sqns.

27.07.41   P/O Warren V. **SHENK**   CAN./J.15072   (US)/RCAF   **Z3317**   IIB   -

Collided with Z3422 over Lincoln and abandoned. American from Pennsylvania, who had joined the sqn early in the month. Later left the squadron for a multi-engine training program and returned to Canada. Didn't transfer to USAAF and later served with No.443 (RCAF) Sqn in Europe.

Note on the aircraft:TOC No.29 MU 27.04.41. Issued No.121 Sqn 04.07.41.

        Sgt Bradley **SMITH**   CAN./R.67550   (US)/RCAF   **Z3422**   IIB   -

As above. American from New York, he was a founder member of the squadron. Left in April 1942 and returned to Canada.

Note on the aircraft:TOC No.22 MU 01.06.41. Issued No.121 Sqn 04.07.41.

15.09.41   P/O Earl W. **MASON**   CAN./J.15009   (US)/RCAF   **Z3667**   IIB   †

Dived into ground while doing aerobatics, 2 m E of Horncasttle, Lincs. American from Minnesota who had joined the squadron during May.

Note on the aircraft:TOC No.18 MU 21.06.41. Issued No.121 Sqn 04.07.41.

SPITFIRE

08.01.42   P/O Jack D. **GILLILAND**   RAF No.106510   (US)/RAF   **W3240**   AV-X   VB   †

Took off at 09.00 with 11 others to proceed to Martlesham Heath for convoy patrol, F/L Kennard leading. Some time after take-off, the weather was judged to be too bad and the formation returned home. P/O Gilliland got lost and crashed in a street in Ipswich. He is believed to have mistaken the fog for cloud. American from Illinois, who had joined the squadron in October 1941.

Note on the aircraft:TOC No.8 MU 18.05.41. Presentation aircraft 'CITY OF LEEDS II'. Issued No.121 Sqn 04.11.41. Previously served with No.609 Sqn.

23.06.42   P/O Julian M. **OSBORNE**   RAF No.112312   (US)/RAF   **BL490**   AV-P   VB   -

During low flying practice with five others, hit the Blackwater River off Osea Ils, Essex. Picked up by fishing boats. Pilot from Virginia, who had joined the unit in May 1942. Transferred to USAAF in September 1942.

Note on the aircraft: TOC No.24 MU 12.12.41. Issued No.121 Sqn 06.05.42. Previosuly with Nos.134 & 81 Sqns.

MAGISTER

10.04.42   Sgt William P. **KELLY**   CAN./R.89902   (US)/RCAF   **T9832**   I   -
Badly damaged as result of a heavy landing after a local flying. Had joined the sqn the month previous. Hailing from New York State, he transferred to the USAAF in September 1942. Crashed into the sea and killed in his Spitfire on 25.02.43, with 4th FG, while strafing a heavily armed German convoy.

Note on the aircraft: TOC No.9 MU 15.08.40. Issued No.121 Sqn 28.05.41 from No.46 Sqn.

Total: 8
including 7 combat aircraft

APPENDIX VII
Aircraft serial numbers matching with individual letters

AV-A
Z3666 (*Hurricane II*)
AB974, AB975 (*Spitfire V*)
AV-B
Z3171 (*Hurricane II*)
AV-C
Z3399 (*Hurricane II*)
P8035 (*Spitfire II*)
AD498 (*Spitfire V*)
AV-D
AA871 (*Spitfire V*)
AV-E
Z5058 (*Hurricane II*)
AD511 (*Spitfire V*)
AV-F

AV-G
Z3670 (*Hurricane II*)
AV-H
W3711 (*Spitfire V*)
AV-I
P8339 (*Spitfire V*)

AV-J
Z3076, Z3596 (*Hurricane II*)
AD289, BM405 (*Spitfire V*)
AV-K
AA922, BM590 (*Spitfire V*)
AV-L
Z5137 (*Hurricane II*)
AV-M
AP521 (*Hurricane II*)
P8076 (*Spitfire II*)
W3899, AA880 (*Spitfire V*)
AV-N
AA903, AD199 (*Spitfire V*)
AV-O

AV-P
P7985 (*Spitfire II*)
AD324, AD460, BL490, BM581 (*Spitfire V*)
AV-Q
P8794, BM578 (*Spitfire V*)
AV-R
Z3427 (*Hurricane II*)
AD548 (*Spitfire V*)

AV-S
Z3770 (*Hurricane II*)
P8136 (*Spitfire II*)
AD471, BL597 (*Spitfire V*)
AV-T
Z3401 (*Hurricane II*)
P8133 (*Spitfire II*)
BL286 (*Spitfire V*)
AV-U

AV-V
Z3643 (*Hurricane II*)
BL239 (*Spitfire V*)
AV-W
P8657 (*Spitfire II*)
AA904, EN768 (*Spitfire V*)
AV-X
Z3239 (*Hurricane II*)
W3240, EN918 (*Spitfire V*)
AV-Y

AV-Z
Z3653 (*Hurricane II*)
P7603 (*Spitfire II*)

APPENDIX VIII
LIST OF KNOWN PILOTS POSTED OR ATTACHED TO THE SQUADRON

RAF
F.E. **ALMOS**, RAF No.67578, *USA*
E.D. **BEATIE**, RAF No.116468, *USA*
C.O. **BODDING**, RAF No.108628, *USA*
D.E. **BOOTH**, RAF No.100984, *USA*
F.R. **BOYLES**, RAF No.111571, *USA*
R.V. **BROSSMER**, RAF No.106352, *USA*
J.I. **BROWN**, RAF No.101456, *USA*
J.A. **CAMPBELL** III, RAF No.64859, *USA*
G. **CARPENTER** JR., RAF No.102636, *USA*
F.M. **COX**, RAF No.103468, *USA*
W.J. **DALEY**, RAF No.101457, *USA*

F.P. **DOWLING**, RAF No.100515, *USA*
B.C. **DOWNS**, RAF No.108631, *USA*
J.G. **DUFOUR** (*a.k.a* J.J. Crowley), RAF No.89765, *USA*
J.E. **DURHAM**, RAF No.61923, *USA*
S.R. **EDNER**, RAF No.64860, *USA*
P.M. **ELLINGTON**, RAF No.115967, *USA*
R.W. **EVANS**, RAF No.108632, *USA*
G.B. **FETROW**, RAF No.113977, *USA*
F.M. **FINK**, RAF No.88385, *USA*
R.W. **FREIBERG**, RAF No.110340, *USA*
F.A. **GAMBLE**, RAF No.101459, *USA*

D. **GEFFENE**, RAF No.64861, *USA*
J.D. **GILLILAND**, RAF No.106510, *USA*
G.O. **HALSEY**, RAF No.112619, *USA*
J.R. **HAPPEL**, RAF No.116161, *USA*
C.A. **HARDIN**, RAF No.113876, *USA*
K.LeR. **HOLDER**, RAF No.118173, *USA*
J.LaR. **KEARNEY**, RAF No.113954, *USA*
H.C. **KENNARD**, RAF No.40396
L.L. **LAUGHLIN**, RAF No.61925, *USA*
J.J. **LYNCH**, RAF No.103470, *USA*
J.B. **MAHON**, RAF No.108640, *USA*
N. **MARANZ**, RAF No.86617, *USA*

C.L. **Martin**, RAF No.65975, *USA*
C.W. **McColpin**, RAF No.61926, *USA*
R.E. **McHan**, RAF No.100991, *USA*
D.W. **McLeod**, RAF No.103466, *USA*
G.H. **Middleton**, RAF No.112311, *USA*
E.T. **Miluck**, RAF No.61928, *USA*
C.C. **Mize**, RAF No.61929, *USA*
H.T. **Nash**, RAF No.121440, *USA*
L.D. **O'Brien**, RAF No.112321, *USA*
J.M. **Osborne**, RAF No.112312, *USA*
C.V. **Padgett**, RAF No.121230, *USA*
V.A. **Parker**, RAF No.100527, *USA*
J.E. **Peck**, RAF No.103471, *USA*
R.P.R. **Powell**, RAF No.33278
L.F. **Reed**, RAF No.61931, *USA*
D.H. **Ross**, RAF No.605410, *USA*
F. **Scudday**, RAF No.61932, *USA*
LeR.A. **Skinner**, RAF No.101460, *USA*
J.T. **Slater**, RAF No.116465, *USA*
F.C. **Smith**, RAF No.109903, *USA*
F.D. **Smith**, RAF No.112305, *USA*

K.G. **Smith**, RAF No.116164, *USA*
F.J. **Smolinsky**, RAF No.605378, *USA*
R.S. **Sprague**, RAF No.103412, *USA*
A.C. **Stanhope**, RAF No.1385981, *USA*
M.L. **Stepp**, RAF No.67579, *USA*
B.A. **Taylor**, RAF No.112307, *USA*
J.LaR. **Taylor**, RAF No.110338, *USA*
T.H. **Tucker**, RAF No.64867, *USA*
J.W. **Warner**, RAF No.65977, *USA*
V.E. **Watkins**, RAF No.64868, *USA*
D.K. **Willis**, RAF No.105136, *USA*
D.A. **Young**, RAF No.114112, *USA*
N.D. **Young**, RAF No.116163, *USA*

RCAF
T.W. **Allen**, Can./J.15015, *USA*
F.C. **Austin**, Can./R.58580, *USA*
L. McF. **Blanding**, Can./R.79288, *USA*
N.R. **Chap**, Can./J.16637, *USA*
G.C. **Daniel**, Can./J.15016, *USA*

P.J. **Fox**, Can./R.99663, *USA*
J.E. **Griffin**, Can./J.15114, *USA*
C.P. **Grimm**, Can./J.15528, *USA*
W.L.C. **Jones**, Can./J.15052, *USA*
W.P. **Kelly**, Can./J.15657, *USA*
C.H. **Marcus**, Can./R.80799, *USA*
H.F. **Marting**, Can./J.4919, *USA*
E.W. **Mason**, Can./J.15009, *USA*
J.J. **Mooney**, Can./J.15014, *USA*
R.F. **Patterson**, Can./J.2928, *USA*
R.G. **Patterson**, Can./R.10134, *USA*
J.M. **Sanders**, Can./J.15658, *USA*
W.V. **Shenk**, Can./J.15072, *USA*
N.D. **Sintetos**, Can./R.82804, *USA*
B. **Smith**, Can./J.15010, *USA*
H.L. **Stewart**, Can./J.15014, *USA*
C.R. **Thorpe**, Can./J.15127, *USA*
R.F. **Tilley**, Can./J.15011, *USA*
F.R. **Vance**, Can./R.80721, *USA*

APPENDIX IX
ROLL OF HONOUR
✝

AIRCREW

Name	Service No	Rank	Age	Origin	Date	Serial
ALLEN, Thomas Willcase	Can./J.15015	F/L	27	(US)/RCAF	31.05.42	W3645
AUSTIN, Frederick Carlton	Can./R.58580	F/Sgt	*n/k*	(US)/RCAF	17.04.42	AD498
BODDING, Cral Olaf	RAF No.108628	P/O	27	(US)/RAF	28.04.42	AD289
BROSSMER, Robert Vincent	RAF No.106352	P/O	27	(US)/RAF	04.05.42	AD460
FREIBERG, Ralph William	RAF No.110340	P/O	31	(US)/RAF	04.05.42	P8794
GILLILAND, Jack Dewberry	RAF No.106510	P/O	22	(US)/RAF	08.01.42	W3240
HOLDER, Kenneth LeRoy	RAF No.118173	P/O	27	(US)/RAF	12.12.41	AA871
LAUGHLIN, Loran Lee	RAF No.61925	P/O	29	(US)/RAF	21.06.41	P3097
MASON, Earl Wallace	Can./J.15009	P/O	24	(US)/RCAF	15.09.41	Z3667
MOONEY, John Joseph	Can./J.15024	F/L	21	(US)/RCAF	16.06.42	W3841
PATTERSON, Richard Fuller	Can./J.2928	P/O	26	(US)/RCAF	07.12.41	W3711
SLATER, John Tassie*	RAF No.116465	P/O	24	(US)/RAF	21.09.42	P8339
TAYLOR, James LaRue	RAF No.110338	P/O	28	(US)/RAF	19.08.42	AD569
YOUNG, Norman Dudley	RAF No.116163	P/O	26	(US)/RAF	31.07.42	AA732

As per 121 ORB as Slater is offically a USAAF loss as O-885133, having made his transfer on 16 September.

Total: 14
United States: 14

GROUNDCREW

Name	Service No	Rank	Age	Origin	Date	Serial
BROOKER, Douglas	RAF No.1454439	AC2	18	RAF	17.03.42	-

Total: 1
United Kingdom: 1

n/k: not known

As was the case with many fighter squadrons formed during 1941, Eagle pilots worked up and commenced operations on Hawker Hurricanes. Above Z3427/AV-R in which 'Sel' Edner shared a victory with John Mooney on 8 August 1941. Below: No.121 Squadron transitioned to the Spitfire in October 1941 using, for a short time, war-weary Spitfire Mk.II's. It then received the more capable Mk.V, which it operated until the squadron was disbanded. Here a crudely repainted AV-S/P8136 features the new camouflage, which was introduced in August 1941. Note the serial painted under the stabilizators.

Above: Spitfire Mk.V BM581/AV-P, usually flown by William Kelly from New York State, seen after being damaged by flak on 21 July 1942. Kelly transferred to the USAAF in September 1942 and was killed in action the following February, being one of the last Spitfire losses sustained by the 4th FG. *(Author's collection)*
Below: No.121 Squadron soldiered on Spitfires Mk.V for the last ten months of its brief existence. Here a very well-known photo showing BM590/AV-R, christened 'Olga', in flight. It was regularly flown by Pilot Officer Gilbert O. Halsey from Oklahoma, who joined the squadron in February 1942. At age 32 Halsey was the oldest Eagle pilot when he transferred to the USAAF in September 1942. He remained with the 335th FS until the end of his tour.

Two founder members of the squadron posing with their respective Hurricanes during the summer 1941. Above, Richard F. Patterson of Virginia posing in Hurricane Z3171/AV-B who, in December 1941, was the first squadron pilot to be killed in action. Below, Reade F. Tilley of Florida posing in front of his Hurricane AV-F named 'Smocky Joe' (probably Z3669). Frustrated by the British climate and seeking more action he chose to serve overseas and fought brilliantly with No.126 Sqn over Malta during 1942. He returned to the United Kingdom in August 1942 with seven confirmed victories and a DFC. Two months later he transferred to the USAAF but did not fly on operations again.

Above: Squadron in August 1942 shortly before becoming the 335th FS, USAAF:
Pilot Officer J.M. Osborne from Virginia shares his experience of a 'dog fight', following a fighter sweep, with other members of the Eagle Squadron, following a fighter sweep. Left to right are: Pilot Officer F.D. Smith from Texas, Flight Sergeant J.M. Sanders from Tennessee, Pilot Officer D.A.Young from Kansas, Pilot Officer Osborne, Squadron Leader W.D. Williams (RAF), Pilot Officer C.V. Padget from Maryland, Pilot Officer G.B. Fetrow from California, Sergeant F.R. Vance from Washington D.C., Pilot Officer G.O. Halsey from Oklahoma, Pilot Officer F.R. Boyles born in Burma (with the cigarette and a shoulder badge 'U.S.A.' instead of the usual Eagle badge), Flight Lieutenant S.R. Edner from Minnesota (just visible), Flight Lieutenant W.J. Daley from Texas, Pilot Officer J.R. Happel from New Jersey, and Pilot Officer J.B. Mahon from California (PoW 19.08.42).
Three were later killed whilst serving USAAF, Fred Boyles, 'Jim' Daley, 'Sel' Edner (post-war), while 'Snuffy' Smith became a prisoner. Fred Vance who remained with the RAF, was killed in action over Sicily in July 1943.

Right :
Jackson B. Mahon who hailed from California, arrived at squadron in December 1941. He became one of the most successful pilots of the unit, by claiming a brace of kills, two double kills in 10 days. On 19 August 1942, during the Dieppe raid, he was able to shoot down his fifth opponent but was shot down himself and thus prevented from lodging a claim. He was however picked up by the Germans and made a prisoner, during which time he was awarded a DFC. After the war he returned to California, where he became the personal pilot and eventually the manager of Errol Flynn, and spent the rest of his career in the movie business.

Above:
Of the four DFCs awarded to 121 Squadron, three went to Americans including 'Jim' Daley from Texas (left) and Selden Edner from Minnesota (right in USAAF uniform). Daley became the CO of the newly formed 335th FS, when he transferred to the USAAF in September 1942. He was subsequently killed in flying accident on 10.09.44 in P-47D-26-RA, 42-28426, while serving with the 371st FG, in Europe, during a second tour of operations. 'Sel' Edner, the squadron's only ace, also transferred to the USAAF in September and eventually became a prisoner of war on 8 March 1944. He remained with the USAAF only to be executed as a member of the American Military Assistance and Advisory Group (MAAG), during the Greek Civil War in January 1949.
Left, Two pilots conversing after returning from a mission, John Mooney from New York (left) and Don McLeod from Massachussetts. Mooney, a key pilot, was earmarked for higher honours and would likely have become CO, if he had not been killed in action as a Flight Commander on 16 June 1942. McLeod, like Reade Tilley, left the squadron in March 1942, for Malta, where he was severely wounded in combat. He returned to the United Kingdom at the end of July 1942 and transferred to the USAAF in September but did not serve with the 4th FG.

Fortunes of war did not offer the same fate to other No.121 Squadron members. Above, Donald K. 'D.K.' Willis from Indiana joined the squadron in June 1942. Before enlisting in the RAF, he had volunteered to serve with the Finnish Air Force in 1939 and flew Bulldogs against the Soviets. He then left for Norway in March 1940 to fly for the Norwegian Navy. A few weeks later the Germans invaded the country and Willis had to flee to the United Kingdom this time, in a twin-engined Heinkel 115 float-plane which had had fallen into Norwegian hands. Unfortunately, he burst an eardrum in September 1942 and his career as an Eagle was stopped. When he recovered No.121 Squadron had become 335th FS with which he continued to fly Spitfires until March 1943. Soon after the squadron had switched to Thunderbolts, he was posted to HQ 8th AF and later to 67th Fighter Wing flying P-38 Lightnings. On 10.04.44 while flying P-38J-10-LO 42-68077 of the 55th FS/20th FG, the fuel pressure was lost due to mechanical failure obliging him to make an emergency forced-landing in Holland. However, Willis evaded capture and finally arrived back in England in June. He never flew operationally again and left the Air Force in 1953.

Below left, Roy W. Evans from Missouri served with the squadron for ten months from December 1941 to September 1942 when he transferred to the USAAF. He claimed his first success in November when still flying Spitfires and added four more while flying Thunderbolts. He became CO of the 335th in August 1943 and left the Group in February 1944 at the end of his tour. He returned in combat a year later with 359th FG flying P-51 Mustangs. On 14 February, his P-51D-15-NA 44-14894 was hit by flak and shot down. He was seriously injured and captured spending the rest of war in hospital. He remained with the USAF after the war eventually retiring as a Colonel. Fonzo D. Smith (below right) from Texas also became an ace while flying with the USAAF. He joined the squadron in May 1942 and transferred in September and flew with the 335th until December. He returned to the 4th FG next spring flying Thunderbolts and shot down his first of his five and a half kills on 22 June. On 03.08.44, his P-51D-5-NA 44-13934 suffered mechanical trouble and was obliged to bale out becoming a PoW until the end of War. (*Author's collection*)

Above left:

Another Smith was serving at the same time as Fonzo Smith. Kenneth G. Smith from Idaho arrived at the squadron in August 1942 flew only few missions with 121 before transferring to the USAAF the following month to the new 4th Fighter Group. Up to March 1944 he shot down five enemy aircraft eventually becoming an ace. On 12.03.44 he ran out of luck and was shot down his P-51B-5-NA 43-6803 was hit by flak. He spent the rest of the war as a PoW and remained in the USAAF after the war. He became the OC of the 37th FG and was killed in a flying accident on 20.10.47 (P-47N-25-RE 44-89399).

Above right, Frank M. Fink who joined the squadron at the end of August 1942 at the same time as Kenneth Smith, and like him, he transferred to the USAAF the following month. However, he had a shorter career when he was obliged to abandon his aircraft (P-47C-5-RE 41-6328) near Paris after mechanical trouble and made a PoW on 09.09.43. After the War he stayed with the USAAF to be killed in a flying accident on 18.06.46 in AT-6F-NT 44-82045.

Aubrey C. Stanhorpe was an unusual case as he was born in France to a French mother and American father, who was a Calavlry officer. He was raised in France serving in the French Air Force during 1939-1940. When France fell he fled to the UK and enlisted with the Free French. In spring 1941 he joined the RAF, however, and upon completing his training, joined 121 in June 1942, transferring to the USAAF the following September. A year later on 07.09.43, he was shot down in his P-47C-2-RE 43-6207 and became a prisoner camp until the end of the war. He is credited with three confirmed victories all with the USAAF. He remained with the USAAF until 1967 and retired as a Lieutenant-Colonel.

Frank R. Boyles (bottom left) was born in Burma of American parents and was still living there when he enlisted in the RAF. He first served with No.234 Sqn in March 1942 before joining No.133 Sqn, the third Eagle squadron in May, moving to 121 in June. Unfortunately he was killed in action on 08.04.44 flying P-51B-5-NA 43-7098 during an escort mission to Brunswick.

Not all Eagle pilots transferred in September 1942, however. Norman Chap (below) from Illinois served with 121 from December 1941 to April 1942 when he volunteered to serve in North Africa where he joined No.250 Sqn from which he was posted missing in action on 07.11.42 - Kittyhawk III FR268.

Leon McF 'Lum' Blanding from South Carolina enlisted in the RCAF in March 1941 and was awarded his flying badge in December that year. A week later he sailed to the United Kingdom and completed his training at No.52 OTU. In May 1942, he was posted to No.165 Sqn but the following month he joined No.121 Sqn and participated to the Dieppe raid on 19.08.42 during which he claimed one FW-190 as a probable. In September he transferred to the USAAF and continued to fly with the 335th FS during the next two years and eventually became the OC of the 335 in June 1944. In July, he was appointed deputy commander of the 4th FG. On 08.08.44, while on a strafing mission over Norway, he was seriously wounded in the head, arm and legs. Despite his wounds he managed to get back to base, but his flying career was over.

Right:
The groundcrew like Douglas Brooker are often forgotten. He joined the squadron in February as a flight mechanic but he was killed at North Weald on 17.03.42 when he was hit by an American truck. He was just 18 years old.
(via Keith Brooker)

SUMMARY OF THE OPERATIONAL ACTIVITY
No.121 (EAGLE) SQUADRON

A/C types	First sortie	Last sortie	Total sorties	Tot Sub-type	Lost Ops	Lost Acc	A/C lost	Claims	V-1	Pilot †	PoWs	Eva.
HURRICANE I	-	-	-	-	-	2	**2**	-	-	**1**	-	-
HURRICANE II	**02.08.41**	**16.10.41**	325	**325**	1	3	**4**	**2.0**	-	**1**	-	-
SPITFIRE II	**01.11.41**	**17.11.41**	57	**57**	-	-	**-**	-	-	**-**	-	-
SPITFIRE V	**16.11.41**	**27.09.42**	2,749	**2,749**	21	2	**23**	**24.0**	-	**12**	**3**	-
Others												
MAGISTER	-	-	-	-	-	1	**1**	-	-	-	-	-
OTHER CAUSES	-	-	-	-	-	-	-	-	-	-	-	-
COMPILATION	**02.08.41**	**27.09.42**		**3,131**	**22**	**8**	**30**	**26.0**	-	**14**	**3**	-

MAIN AWARDS

DSO: -

DFC: 4

DFM: -

Points of interest:
- Second of the three squadrons formed with American volunteers.

Unsolved mystery:

Statistics:
- Lost one aircraft every 142 sorties [Hurricane I: -, Hurricane II: 355, Spitfire II: -, Spitfire V: 130]
- 24.00 % of the combat aircraft losses occurred during non operational flights.

BADGE
An Indian warrior's head with head-dress.

The badge implies the squadron's association with the U.S.A.

MOTTO
FOR LIBERTY

Authority: King George VI, September 1942

Hawker Hurricane Mk.IIB Z3427, Pilot Officer Caroll W. McColpin (USA), Kirton-in-Lindsey, Summer 1941.
Taken on charge on 07.06.41, Z3427 was issued to No.121 Sqn the following month on 04.07.41 and coded AV-E. It became the personal mount of Pilot Officer 'Red' McColpin until he left the squadron for No.71 (Eagle) Sqn early in September 1941. However it was this aircraft Pilot Officer 'Sel' Edner was flying when he shared a confirmed victory on 08.08.41 with Jack Mooney, the first claim of the squadron. Z3427 left the squadron on 30.10.41 whilst the unit was converting to Spitfire Mk.IIs.

Supermarine Spitfire Mk.IIA P8136, Kirton-in-Lindsey, November 1941.
This aircraft is a kind of mystery for the squadron. Taken of charge on 30.03.41 and a presentation aircraft 'ALDERSHOT' but sometimes named 'THE CAT', an unofficial name. He served with No.65 Sqn and later with No.411 (RCAF) Sqn and later with No.340 (French) Sqn at the end of November 1941. However, the individual movement card of this aircraft shows no trace of its use by No.121 Sqn, but the ORB and logbooks confirm that P8136 was indeed used by the squadron. The aircraft was one of the first two Spitfire Mk.IIBs collected directly from No.411 Sqn at Digby where it was coded DB-S. It was bring back by the CO himself, Squadron Leader Powell on 17.10.41. On the ORB, more than a dozen flights are recorded until 12.11.41. Being used mainly to transitione to the Spitfire Mk.V, no Spitfire Mk.II was allocated to a specific pilot.Note that the new camouflage Dark Green/Ocean Grey has been crudely painted on the aircraft and the serial has been painted under the stabilisators.

Supermarine Spitfire Mk.VB W3711, Pilot Officer Richard F. Patterson (USA), Kirton-in-Lindsey, December 1941.

Taken of charge on 18.08.41, this aircraft served first with No.603 Sqn before being issued to No.121 Sqn on 7 November 1941 as among the first Mk.Vs received by the squadron and it became the mount of Pilot Officer Richard 'Pat' Patterson of Virginia who had join the squadron in June 1941. Dices and an ace of spade were painted on the fuselage band just above the serial. It was in this aircraft 'Pat' Patterson was killed in action on 7 December 1941, being the first killed in action of the squadron.

Supermarine Spitfire Mk.VB BM405, Pilot Officer Jackson B. Mahon (USA), Southend, June 1942.

Taken of charge on 03.04.42, it was issued to No.121 Sqn on 17.06.42 to replace one of the many losses sustained by the squadron in April and May 1942. Believed to have been coded AV-J which was used by AD289 lost previously, it became the mount of Pilot 'Barry' Mahon (before that he didn't have any aircraft allocated) on which he made one of two double claims, on 31 July and before to be eventually was shot down while flying this aircraft during the Dieppe raid. On the aircraft are painted the first two 'kills' he claim on 8 June 1942. Surprisingly the Squadron's diarist continued to transcript AD289 in Form 541 during the next few weeks, being probably confused by the same individual letter generating confusion in the aircraft flown by 'Barry' Mahon and AD289 is reputadly to be the aircraft 'Barry' was flying when he made his first two 'kills' on 08.06.42 but AD289 has been lost on the previous 28.04.42.

Supermarine Spitfire Mk.VB BM590, Pilot Officer Gilbert O. Halsey (USA), Southend, July 1942.

Taken on charge on 25.04.42, this aircraft was issued to No.121 Sqn at a date which not recorded on its movement card but the firt trace of this aircraft can be found on 25.06.42. BM590/AV-R, christened 'Olga' was regularly flown by Pilot Officer Gilbert O. Halsey from Oklahoma, who joined the squadron in February 1942 and claimed a probable aircraft destroyed over Dieppe on 19.08.42.

Supermarine Spitfire Mk.VB BM581, Pilot Officer William P. Kelly (USA), Southend, July 1942.

Taken of charge on 24.06.42, this aircraft was issued to No.121 Sqn on 28 June and became the mount of Pilot Officer William P. Kelly of New York State who joined the squadron in March 1942. He choose as personal artwork, an Uncle SAm's hat inside a circle of white stars. He was flying this aircraft when it received several hits from ground fire on 21July during a sweep over Holland. Returned to service after repairs, it continued to fly with the squadron and later on with the new 335th FS as AV-K until April 1943 when it was returned to RAF as the 4th FG had completed his convertion to P-47.

www.ingramcontent.com/pod-product-compliance
Lightning Source LLC
LaVergne TN
LVHW072123070426

835511LV00002B/76